BOOK ANALYSIS

Written by Leonie Cater

Cat on a Hot Tin Roof

BY TENNESSEE WILLIAMS

BrightSummaries.com

TENNESSEE WILLIAMS

AMERICAN PLAYWRIGHT

- **Born in Columbus, Mississippi (United States) in 1911.**
- **Died in New York, New York (United States) in 1983.**
- **Notable works:**
  - *A Streetcar Named Desire* (1947), play
  - *The Glass Menagerie* (1944), play
  - *Suddenly Last Summer* (1958), play

Amongst the most celebrated playwrights of 20th-century American drama, Tennessee Williams left his mark on literary history with his enthralling, tension-ridden oeuvre, dealing with themes as diverse and polemic as human sexuality, human relations and communications, homosexuality, social conventions and mental health. Several autobiographical details in his work have been identified and explored by critics, demonstrating that the writer drew on real life and his lived experiences in his creative processes. Parallels have been drawn, for example, between *The Glass Menagerie*'s Laura and Amanda Wingfield, and Williams' own sister and mother, respectively. It was this very play, in fact, that catapulted the playwright's career to the lofty heights of success, cementing his standing amongst such playwrights as Eugene O'Neill (1888-1953) and Arthur Miller (1915-2005). His career entered a period of steady decline later in life due to increased drug and alcohol use. This decrease in the popularity of his plays has also been attributed to Williams' attempt at a new style. He died on 25 February 1983 aged 71, having choked to death on a plastic bottle cap.

CAT ON A HOT TIN ROOF

20TH-CENTURY AMERICAN DRAMA

- **Genre:** play
- **Reference edition:** Williams, T. (2009) *Cat on a Hot Tin Roof*. London: Penguin Modern Classics. [Kindle Edition].
- **1st edition:** 1955
- **Themes:** human emotion, communication, marginalisation, sexuality, homosexuality, misogyny

An exploration of the extremes of human emotion, Williams' prize-winning drama explores one closeted gay man's internalized homophobia and self-disgust, and the consequences this has for him and the rest of his family, including his wife. It was written in the 1950s, when homosexuality and homophobia were still relatively new topics to the mainstream American media, and Williams utilizes his play both to speak out on this important topic and to offer insight into the failings and importance of human communication. Despite the controversial subject matter, the play was a major success upon its premiere and continues to be studied in classrooms and lecture halls today. And although we may have come a long way since the 1950s, the ideas and themes explored in the work remain of utmost importance in modern, 21st-century society.

SUMMARY

ACT ONE

Curtains open to a 'bed-sitting-room' in a house on a Mississippi plantation. The audience is plunged into an everyday interaction between an apparently highly-strung married couple on a summer evening. The wife, Margaret, complains to her husband, Brick, about the antics of "Gooper's kiddies" (loc. 165) who, it transpires, are the children of Brick's brother and his wife, Mae. Margaret reveals that Gooper and Mae are conspiring to block Brick from his rightful inheritance – and that Brick's father is dying of cancer, which appears to be of secondary importance to Margaret. Brick's alcoholism is revealed to the audience by Margaret, and it appears that this is the key to Gooper and Mae's plan: to play upon Brick's drinking problem, as well as Margaret's apparent inability to conceive, to have him declared an unfit inheritor. Soon, doubts are cast on Margaret's 'inability' and it comes to light that Brick is no longer intimate with her. She remains devoted to her husband, even though he implores her to take a lover. Brick continues drinking, in pursuit of the "click" (loc. 401) he so needs before he can reach a state of calm, while Margaret explains the importance of the upcoming birthday party for Big Daddy Pollitt, Brick's father. Brick's mother, Big Mama, enters the room. She comes bearing seemingly good news, being under the impression that her husband tested negative for cancer and has instead been diagnosed with a "spastic colon" (loc. 555). However, this is a lie which has been told to Big Mama and Big Daddy to spare the birthday celebrations.

The conversation between Big Mama and Margaret turns to Margaret's supposed failings as a wife, with her mother-in-law chastising her for turning Brick to the bottle, a claim vehemently contested by Margaret. She departs, leaving Margaret alone in the room. Brick enters and she turns on him, expounding the amount of men who *are* interested in her. The conversation turns monetary once again as Margaret claims she does not have the money to leave even if she wanted to, leading her back to the importance of his father's will. The conversation turns to a discussion about a man named Skipper, Brick's dead friend who, according to Margaret, entertained the idea of a non-platonic relationship between the two men, much to Brick's supposed disgust. It transpires that Margaret once confronted Skipper, leading to a violent altercation between the two and, ultimately, attempted intercourse as Skipper tried to prove the inaccuracy of Margaret's claims. As she continues to discuss the matter, Brick becomes violent, and hurls his crutch at her. One of Gooper's children, Dixie, enters the room, putting an end to the altercation.

ACT TWO

Nothing has changed since the end of Act One. With Brick on crutches due to a broken ankle – which occurred during a drunken, late-night stint on the Athletics field – Big Daddy's birthday celebration is to take place in their room. The guests enter and the party begins. There is music from the Hi-Fi, cruel jokes from Big Daddy at Big Mama's expense, and overflowing joy from Big Mama about her husband's supposed negative test for cancer. This odd 'party' atmosphere soon comes a halt, however, as tensions begin to rise – both between Mae and Margaret and between Big Daddy and Mama Pollitt, to the point that Big Daddy accuses his wife of secretly harbouring a desire to take over his plantation.

The next instance of tension takes place between Big Daddy and Brick. Concerned about his son's alcoholism, Big Daddy attempts to get to the root of the problem and have a real conversation about Brick's issues, and his compulsion to drink until the 'click'. After rambling for a while about his travels around Europe and his new zest for life after supposedly receiving the all-clear for cancer, eventually Big Daddy becomes exasperated by his son's cool reticence. He grabs Brick's crutch out from under him, using it as a bargaining chip in exchange for information on his drinking problem. Eventually Brick concedes that the root cause of his alcoholism is "DISGUST!" (loc. 1461). He is reluctant to reveal the cause of this sentiment, or where this disgust is directed. After further rambling from Big Daddy about the importance of Brick pulling his life together and taking over the estate, the pair return to the subject at hand, leading Big Daddy to mention the influence of Skipper's death on Brick, citing this as the start of Brick's drinking. This breaks through Brick's cool demeanour, inciting a degree of anger and discomfort we only saw briefly in the similar previous interaction between him and Margaret on the same topic. He begins to shout hysterically, expressing his horror at his father's implication that he is a "ducking sissy" (loc. 1654), a "queer" (*ibid.*) and a "fairy" (loc. 1682) – Brick's words. Eventually, Brick explains his version of the story, claiming that Margaret planted the idea in Skipper's head that he harboured a secret sexual desire for Brick. Skipper then attempted to sleep with Margaret to prove that this was not true. The encounter failed, leading Skipper to believe that he was, in fact, homosexual. Brick finishes his story by explaining that he received a drunken phone call from Skipper one night wherein he made some kind of confession to Brick, and that was the last time they talked until his death.

Big Daddy can see the gaps in the story and is frustrated by his son's inability to be honest with his father. He begins to chastise him over his "mendacity" (loc. 1579), leading Brick to hint at Big Daddy's positive cancer tests, causing Big Daddy to spiral mentally, overwhelmed by this apparent revelation. He leaves the stage shouting, "CHRIST – DAMN – ALL – LYING SONS OF – LYING BITCHES!" (loc. 1801) while Brick remains motionless. The curtain falls.

ACT THREE

With Big Daddy and Brick offstage, the focus returns to the remaining party guests and their awkward, antagonistic interactions. Mae and Gooper attempt to breach the uncomfortable subject of Big Daddy's true cancer diagnosis, with some difficulty due to the dramatics of Big Mama Pollitt – namely her loud refusal to take part in any conversation kept secret from her husband and her fuss over Brick – her "precious baby" (loc. 880) – once he, too, enters. Eventually, however, they manage to successfully confess the truth about the patriarch's condition, leaving Big Mama angry and distraught as she seeks out confirmation from her "only son", Brick (loc. 2616). The revelation leads Big Mama to reveal her desire that Brick should take over the estate if he can straighten himself out, much to the chagrin of Mae and Gooper. As Big Mama's preference for Margaret and Brick becomes increasingly obvious, Mae and Gooper become increasingly infuriated, leading Gooper to show his true colours and vested financial interest in his father's demise. Gooper presents a trusteeship he has drawn up with his partner which hints at his retention of control over his father's estate, further enraging his mother.

Big Mama goes to Brick and initiates a touching mother-son moment, attempting to connect with her favourite, beloved child. She voices her wish for Brick to produce offspring, and subsequently (and conveniently), Margaret announces her own apparent pregnancy. Big Mama bursts into tears of joy and rushes off to tell Big Daddy, while Mae and Gooper cross-examine their sister-in-law, convinced of her 'mendacity'. Soon, the angry couple storm off, leaving Maggie and Brick alone. Maggie reveals that it is her time of the month to conceive, that she has taken Brick's alcohol hostage, and that she will continue to do so until he sleeps with her. Shocked, he reaches for his crutch – but not before it is seized by his wife. Brick has nothing left to say, appearing to give in to her demands. She assures him that she really does love him, to which he simply replies, "Wouldn't it be funny if that was true?" (loc. 2343), echoing his father's previous comment on his own marriage. The curtain falls.

CHARACTER STUDY

BRICK

Brick has all the makings of a conventional, mainstream protagonist. We are told throughout the text of his enviable charm and cool, the favour he has gained from his family, and his good looks. He appears to embody the American masculine ideal – an attractive, athletic football player with apparent sexual attraction and prowess. And yet, from the beginning of the first act, the audience detects that there is something more behind the façade of this archetypal man. His alcoholism is revealed very early on, when Margaret catches us up with the situation at hand, voicing her suspicions that her in-laws are plotting to utilize Brick's drinking problem to exclude him from his father's estate, and send him to the Rainbow Hill rehabilitation centre. This demonstrates Brick's vulnerability, both to whatever mental demons he appears to be facing, and to the very real antagonistic forces of Mae and Gooper. And yet, the reality of his predicament seems either not to occur or not to matter to our leading man. His actions and speech here are described by such stage directions as: "dreamily" (loc. 291), "absently" (loc. 289), "coolly" (loc. 310), "indifferently" (loc. 339), demonstrating a detachment from life, particularly from his wife.

This vulnerability is compounded and embodied by his use of a crutch, following an injury incurred during a drunken night out on the athletic field. This crutch proves important throughout the play in charting the development of his character and of the other characters' responses to him. At various points in the play, for example, either Margaret or Big Daddy will take his crutch from him in order to impose their power over the invalid, and oblige him to follow their orders. This abuse of Brick's crutches escalates from Big Daddy's attempt to make his son tell him about the source of his alcoholism to Margaret's decision to force her husband to have sex with her in order to produce an heir. And in a play in which two of the main characters – Big Daddy and Gooper – can be seen as the embodiment of the ruling patriarchy, Brick's vulnerability becomes all the more evident.

Of course, the source of this vulnerability is his extreme discomfort with his own sexuality, particularly with regard to his close relationship with his deceased friend, Skipper. While Brick never openly acknowledges his homosexuality, his extreme mood swings upon any mention of the nature of their relationship and his bizarre, nonsensical outbursts when being questioned by his father do appear to confirm this. One such exchange between himself and his father, for example, is as follows:

> "BRICK: When we were touring the country in pro-football an' shared hotel-rooms we'd reach across the space between the two beds and shake hands to say goodnight, yeah, one or two times we –
> BIG DADDY: Brick, nobody thinks that that's not normal!
> BRICK: Well, they're mistaken, it was! It was a pure an' true thing an' that's not normal." (loc. 1688)

Even though his father is reassuring him that such interactions are completely normal, Brick bulldozes straight past any of his father's attempts to show understanding for his situation, and shows intense disgust towards "fairies" (loc. 1682), "ducking sissies" (loc. 1654) or "queers" (*ibid.*). As such, it becomes apparent that Brick has internalised the social conventions and discrimination of 1950s American society, leading to the disgust he feels for himself. He is trapped in a discriminatory prison of his own making.

MARGARET

Beautiful yet miserable, Margaret is trapped in a failed marriage, bound emotionally and financially to a man who does not love her. When the audience is first introduced to the character, their impression of her is not particularly favourable: she appears to be inordinately angered by some playing children, or "no-neck monsters" (loc. 686) as she calls them, due to the fact that "their fat little heads are set on their fat little bodies without a bit of connexion" (loc. 168). "It's too bad because you can't wring their necks if they've got no necks to wring!" (loc. 171) she jokes. And yet as the act advances, the source of her ire becomes clear: tortured by her in-laws' taunts about their inability to conceive, as well as by the fact that her husband refuses to sleep with her, Margaret is extremely unhappy. When describing her predicament to her husband, she declares: "I'm not living with you. We occupy the same cage" (loc. 431). In this way, Margaret becomes a source of pity for the audience, obliging us to be more sympathetic to her plight as she attempts to secure a future for herself and her husband through their acquisition of her father-in-law's estate.

Just as Brick's vulnerability stems from widespread homophobic discrimination in 1950s America, particularly in the Deep South, Margaret is heavily impacted by social conventions of the era pertaining to women. At several moments throughout the play, the couple's inability to conceive is thrown at Margaret as an accusation, as if this were her sole duty. Mae is particularly guilty of this, spouting such remarks as: "Maggie, honey, if you had children of your own you'd know how funny that is" (loc. 446) and "Such a pity that Maggie an' Brick can't oblige!" (loc. 2227) (when Big Mama voices her desire for a grandchild by Brick and Margaret). Big Mama also accuses her of turning Brick to alcohol, once again holding the woman responsible for the actions of her male counterpart. And yet, she handles such social pressure in an entirely opposite way to Brick. Whereas her husband has retreated into his own dreamworld, clouded by excessive alcohol consumption, Margaret is constantly anxious, demonstrated in her constant chatting and plotting, and shown even in her very first stage directions – "a pretty young woman with anxious lines in her face" (loc. 153); "Margaret's voice is both rapid and drawling [...] the lines are almost sung, always continuing a little beyond her breath so she has to gasp for another. Sometimes she intersperses the lines with a little wordless singing, such as 'Da-da-daaaa!'" (loc. 156). In this way, Williams demonstrates the ways in which the two sexes are forced to deal with the challenges of their respective experiences of marginalisation in 1950s America – women through dedicated planning and responsibility so as to ensure successful dependence on their husbands; men through internalisation and silent suffering.

BIG DADDY

'Big Daddy' is the patriarch of the house – and his name alone more than suggests that we should perceive the character as the archetypal patriarchal figure. He relishes discussing his inheritance and massive fortune, and he has every one of his relatives (perhaps aside from Brick) tripping over themselves to fall into his favour – Big Daddy is in control. He enjoys talking about the size and success of his plantation and is hugely misogynistic, making disparaging, demeaning remarks both about the women of the household and women generally. When discussing his new lease of (sexual) life and his plans to be unfaithful to his wife, for example, he announces to his son that he is going to "pick me a choice one, I don't care how much she costs, I'll smother her in – minks! Ha ha! I'll strip her naked and smother her in minks and choke her with diamonds! Ha ha! I'll strip her naked and choke her with diamonds and smother her with minks and hump her from hell to breakfast" (loc. 1337). The image combines violent misogyny with a vulgar display of wealth, truly embodying Big Daddy's 1950s patriarchal character. Coupled with his treatment of his son, removing Brick's crutch in order to blackmail him for information on his alcoholism, his disparaging remarks about his own wife (both behind her back and to her face), and the financial power he exercises over his household, Big Daddy represents an oppressive force in the work.

ANALYSIS

THE PRISON OF THE DEEP SOUTH

As a gay man from America's Deep South, Tennessee Williams would have been no stranger to the isolation of the marginalised figure. At the time the play was written, the topic of homosexuality was only just being breached in mainstream American media and was largely condemned. Similarly, women had only received the right to vote 30 years prior and the sexual revolution of the 1960s was still to come. Essentially, the 1950s remained a hugely repressive period of time for various, sizeable groups of people. As such, the themes Williams appears to evoke in *Cat on a Hot Tin Roof* – misogyny, homosexuality and homophobia, the power of the patriarchy, and freedom of sexual expression – are based on controversial topics of the era. Indeed, when *Cat on a Hot Tin Roof* was adapted into a cinematic box-office hit in 1958, starring Elizabeth Taylor (British-American actress, 1932-2011) and Paul Newman (American actor, 1925-2008), most of the allusions to Brick's homosexuality were eradicated, with the Motion Picture Production Code (film industry guidelines which were applied to most films produced in the United States between 1930 and 1968) playing a large part in this sizeable alteration. Williams was an apparent pioneer, ahead of his time in his critique of homophobia and social conventions.

The work is not just political, however. Although the work allows the playwright to showcase his opinions on important social issues, these topics also permitted Williams to explore, analyse and demonstrate the wide array of human passions, communications and reactions. What better way to represent these extremes of emotion than to play upon controversial contemporary topics? Rejection, isolation, anger, desperation, extreme relief and extreme shock are just some of the many emotions put on display in *Cat on a Hot Tin Roof*, and they all stem from the same central, politicised questions pertaining to male power and sexuality. It is up to the audience to decide whether these high-running emotions are the by-product of treating these prominent, controversial topics, or vice-versa.

SETTING

Williams' work is typically dripping in symbolism, adding further depth to the action as it unfurls onstage, and the set of *Cat on a Hot Tin Roof* is no exception. Indeed, it is no accident that the play takes place in the midst of a hot, southern summer, much like Williams' earlier tension-ridden work *A Streetcar Named Desire.* The playwright has a tendency to use pathetic fallacy, utilizing climate to symbolize and exteriorise running tensions. In this case, these tensions are compounded by the stuffy, claustrophobic nature of the set, with all action taking place in the same room – Brick and Margaret's 'bed-sitting-room'. This is further intensified by the fact that so much of the play revolves around sex: sex that produces children; sex that does not produce children; gay sex; straight sex; no sex – even Big Daddy expresses his own sexual desires. In this way, a hot, summer evening setting in a couple's bedroom intensifies one of the work's predominant themes, literally placing it in centre stage.

Furthermore, the constancy of the set design furthers one of the play's key themes: marginalisation and isolation. Just as Brick has no choice but to keep his sexuality hidden, entrapping himself in a cage of lies and alcoholism, and just as Margaret has no choice but to stick by her husband, both for financial and emotional reasons, the audience is forced to face the same location throughout the entirety of the play. On the one hand, this focuses the spectators' attention to the words and action on stage, for this is the core of Williams' work. On the other, the audience is presented with a tangible sense of Margaret and Brick's claustrophobic predicament. As such, the importance of Williams' set design becomes clear.

Even the set's "weathered wood" (loc. 134) furniture with a "quality of tender light" (*ibid.*) has a specific reason as to its inclusion. As Williams explains in his opening notes for the set designer: "the set is the background for a play that deals with human extremities of emotion, and it needs that softness behind it" (loc. 136). One could also argue that the intense drama on stage – from near-declarations of homosexuality to the revelation of a positive cancer screening – needs to be the focal point for the audience. Additionally, through the use of such muted furniture, any objects truly intended to catch our attention are further highlighted – the "huge console combination of radio-phonograph (Hi-Fi with three speakers), TV set and liquor cabinet" (loc. 140), for example, which Williams tells us is a "very complete and compact little shrine to virtually all the comforts and illusions behind which we hide from such things as the characters in the play are faced with" (loc. 144). Again, just as we saw in the playwright's use of pathetic fallacy and constant scenery, Williams demonstrates a desire to confront his audience with the play's central themes.

THE FAILURE OF COMMUNICATION

At the root of *Cat on a Hot Tin Roof* are, essentially, various breakdowns of communication, faced by each member of the cast at some point in the play's development: Brick is unable to communicate his true feelings to his father or wife, Big Mama Pollitt is unsuccessful in conveying her love for her husband, and Mae and Gooper are frustrated by Big Mama's inability to listen to their opinions and look beyond her favourite son. As Williams writes in his own stage directions: "I'm trying to catch the true quality of experience in a group of people, that cloudy, flickering, evanescent – fiercely charged! – interplay of live human beings in the thundercloud of a common crisis" (loc. 1597). The most obvious example of this is the central scene and conversation between Big Daddy and Brick, and their extraordinary ability to say nothing, and yet, in doing so, reveal everything. For example, Brick's elusive responses to his father's questions about the nature of his relationship with Skipper speak volumes – and Big Daddy Pollitt knows this, as shown in his angry declaration: "That half-assed story!" (loc. 1735).

And just as neither father or son are capable of understanding one another, the men are also incapable of perceiving or understanding their wives' true affection. Williams highlights this by exactly paralleling a phrase of Big Daddy's in Brick's final, closing remark: "Wouldn't it be funny if that was true..." (loc. 2343), a comment which on both occasions is uttered in response to their respective partners' declaration of love. That such lack of understanding is present in both generations suggests that the family's ancestral line is doomed to repeat the same errors in communication over and over – and if we are to take the Pollitt family as a microcosm of human emotion, then this final remark becomes an apparently negative comment on the human condition.

FURTHER REFLECTION

SOME QUESTIONS TO THINK ABOUT...

- What do you make of Williams' treatment of the African American characters? Is their portrayal politicised?
- In what respects is Mae just as much a victim of society as Margaret?
- The themes evoked in *Cat on a Hot Tin Roof* are ahead of Williams' time. Would the play attract as much attention if it were first published today?
- How would you stage the play? Would you include a modern twist?
- Although they are minor characters, Reverend Tooker and Doctor Bauer do appear periodically. What do you make of their inclusion?
- Is knowledge of the play's historical context necessary to grasp its underlying meanings?
- Is there anything you gain from reading a Tennessee Williams play that you lose by watching a performance of it?

We want to hear from you!
Leave a comment on your online library
and share your favourite books on social media!

FURTHER READING

REFERENCE EDITION

- Williams, T. (2009) *Cat on a Hot Tin Roof.* London: Penguin Modern Classics. [Kindle Edition].

REFERENCE STUDIES

- (No date) Tennessee Williams. *Encyclopaedia Britannica*. [Online]. [Accessed 30 November 2018]. Available from: <https://www.britannica.com/biography/Tennessee-Williams>
- Roudané, M.C. (1997) *The Cambridge Companion to Tennessee Williams*. Cambridge: Cambridge University Press.

ADAPTATIONS

- *Cat on a Hot Tin Roof.* (1958) [Film]. Richard Brooks. Dir. USA: Metro-Goldwyn-Mayer.

MORE FROM BRIGHTSUMMARIES.COM

- Reading guide – *A Streetcar Named Desire* by Tennessee Williams.

www.brightsummaries.com

Ebook EAN: 9782808016575

Paperback EAN: 9782808016582

Legal Deposit: D/2018/12603/589

Digital conception by Primento, the digital partner of publishers.

Printed in Great Britain
by Amazon

43952856R00031